VIVID
PARTITIONS

VIVID PARTITIONS

Uri Rosenshine

MADHAT PRESS
CHESHIRE, MASSACHUSETTS

MadHat Press
MadHat Incorporated
PO Box 422, Cheshire, MA 01225

The Library of Congress has assigned
this edition a Control Number of
2022949602

ISBN 978-1-952335-51-8 (paperback)

Words by Uri Rosenshine
Book design by MadHat Press
Cover image: Timnah Rosenshine and JohnClaud Ruder
Author portrait: Keith Roselle

www.madhat-press.com

First Printing

Printed in the United States of America

For Louise

Table of Contents

I

II

I

Lotus

Once, to prove a point
I pedaled a bouquet of lotus flowers
Across Hanoi.

More focused then, the sort of love
I practiced; fewer friends involved,
More action.

*

Autumn days again,
Scenes of contemplation.
Leaving the house to be alone.

It's good to walk
Up and down the street
Below the branches of elms.

*

The school is heating up
As first-years look for sex.
Gathered away together, fagots for a fire.

Dull, painful souvenir.
Was I not wiser once? Purer?
What were my names for things?

The Parrot

You have a house
You wake up, and go
To the window
It is bright, you think
Like a theater

You see cars
And sunlight

You see sparrows
In the tree, and say
Outside, they are poor
And busy

In your house, there is a corner
That you like, next to the mirror
Where you sleep

You're not heavy enough
To play the piano
That's just how it is, you say

Sometimes, you go
To the bookshelf
And chew the spines
I am an admirer
Of good books, you say

At night, you say
The moon is for sleep
And you retire

Each day is the same
You go to the window
This is the world, you say
Adjusting your perch

Bright, like a theater,
Bright

Chagallig

Later that night
the moon was large and blue over the buckwheat

The cat sat beside a samovar
behind the barn window

and the field mouse stood
at the grasses' edge

Listen, then, the train passed
behind the poplars
and the angel, the same one
I told you about before, flew
right over Vitebsk

Our bodies were tall as the barn,
we understood, we were seated, incredulous

We saw nighttime, a history of nighttime:
new odors, frankness in speech
and the distant intelligence
of shoulders

Eternity, that strange bird—
I asked her, asked her if she knew
what I meant by it,
the sky behind her face, behind the moon
spread like a great flag

I knew, then, what country
we were in, whose land

It was obvious—the dream of a city
no taller than a stalk of buckwheat—
how we would have towered over them!

The smallest materials,
beetles, ferns and funguses, several
months' worth of the moon
lying spent on the ridge
of milk jugs emptied
in the square—

We can account for these,
numbering them, one on the other
with our hands and mouths,
in our given fashion,
untutored in the sum of things

I spelled it out on her,
along the grain, you know—

She knew what I had meant to say,
exactly what I meant to say.

Monadology

The library is full of leaves
Blown in whenever anyone
Comes through the doors

Blast of dry air,
Smoke—spruce branches
Piled in a flame

Like the face of that reader
Resting on a sentence of—
What is it, Leibniz?

One and one and one
The burning branches going by

Put copper in his hair
Discernment in his eye

Invitation to Vermont

1.
The blue mountains
and the white river,

a border,
and the too-cold taps
god drinks of there

We'll go up the trail to the drum
of spruces, and the hissing of ships burning,

and later tell about pages of change,
leaves, branches, bark, the cold,
the skeleton of nature—

By car, that dreamy instrument,
the fuse and sparrow,
up from Providence with
fresh arguments: on Virgil,
the acorn, the old edicts of
Mahicans, or Melville in Nuku Hiva
of the Marquesas …

2.
The ship hovers between stars
and the reflection of stars—

the car of the moon
and its charge

Bodily moon, cedar drifting: sheet
drawn out by the wind

Somnus, god of sleep, comes down
to Palinurus, helmsman

and flings him from the deck
into the sea—

as into sleep: swallowed ambiguously
between a void and a light—

and leaves his name to a promontory.

The Tea-Stall

In the newspaper
an avalanche has buried
twenty hikers
in the Himalayas.

A few survived, it says,
by taking cover
at a nearby tea-stall.

The word "residuum"
comes to mind, a chemist's word
but I don't mean it in that way.

Residuum, as if it meant
the destiny of things.

*

You need a scarf,
a good scarf for the winter months,

bags of salt, boxes of tea
and a snow shovel.

A scarf, like a zen koan
you can't remove, except

by meditation. Permanent knot
preserves the wanderer.

11

It gets colder, but you
are dressed in a sheep's costume.

Your sneakers break grass
on the frozen glade.

*

I come down from the mountains
The valley dims
I wander silently and am somewhat unhappy
And my sighs ask, Where?

A solemn code on the piano.
Then the wanderer, a baritone:
Ich komme vom gebirge her ...
and I recognize his inflection

the voice of one
coming to an erasure
a blank place.

But the wanderer grapples with this:

Ich—
Ich—
Ich—

*

Why did we think it would be vacant here,
uniform?

It is dense and varied,
full of partial memories of final things.

The walk to work repeated,
the friends avoided,
the dinner conversation;
the wrestlers on the TV
in the evening.

Sometimes the quietness of things distracts us.
Then we fall again, through the inventory.

*

The umbrellas are open
drying in the hall.

In the window which once
seemed to convey seasons
the landscape has disappeared.

Where sparrows brawled
in the sand,
where grapevines hung
with blistered leaves,
where clouds dissolved—

immersion, fragmentation, disintegration, desiccation,
dispersion ...

*

Nothing is left
except the glass

which reflects
the room

the bed and the desk
yourself

facing a window
to an identical room,

the final identity
of your meditation:

Da ist

Nichts

Nichts

Nichts ...

Modest Forecast

You are in the total force of your flower.
You are a lot of things. Parcels
Upon doorsteps, sparrows
In a boxwood, documents
Issued down from offices,
Officious songs in the mouths
Of loudspeakers; and an audience
Too, the most terrifying.

These geese that fly in October
Strict as axioms doing what they do—

*

They said nothing

Put two cigarettes in his mouth, lit them
And gave him one.
There was a sound of distant thunder
The storm doors in the other room were being closed

Though it was daytime
A light was burning by the bed

Undid a breast button
Lay down on the quilts
Propped on one elbow
Kissed for four or five minutes
Slipped his hand inside

The other boy's tunic, under the button
That was loose.

The sound of the trolley
The sound of the crow of roosters
The sound inappropriate at this time
As if it were the middle of the night

Pine boards, spots
Of coagulated resin in the center
Of the knots were turned by the sun's rays
To the color of blood. A thin beam of light
Glinted off the muddy water that filled the vase in the alcove.

*

The sprinklers came on in the dark courtyard.
The growth of a man takes him after all
Towards not more ability, but less,
A retirement, in which
Ideas come, instinct bringing them.

Which bands are at the bar this October?
Turning right on our street
Straightforward happiness is over.

Oh, you were so right.
You were approaching me,
Pressing against my breast. And then
There was a flowering of something,

A resting and attaching of something
In a sweet rash of generosity and unconcern

Like the Japanese pagoda tree spreading its petals on the stoop
The nectar of which drives the bees out of their minds.

The Surface Circus

The Jewish holiday approaches
I remember things

but not precisely
the things I remember
come back for what they need

is more like it,
like so many ex-girlfriends

we go out, drunk and talkative
New Haven disappoints us tonight, I want to write
still drunk, I try to read your mind,
the circle of your moods,
but have no paper—you shudder,
as someone splashed with water

looking at you I think this through seriously
I also think of skinning the deer in Wisconsin
and the prom-night homicide of that month

whether the senator really did cheat on his wife or
did she set fire to their mattress out of a cruelty
and irritability brought on by the short days and the snow

you are so understanding,
famous, cheerful
I can tell you this story
as if it were informative

when your mood changes
you say something else

and I can laugh or argue it,
there is no difference
we send my sister a picture
of the wooden fish from Bali
smoking a bowl—she and I

plan to smoke before synagogue
in order to be able to fall down and cry
on god's young aerial feet as if he were
an athlete who had spurned us
in favor of a trophy and a life of durable solitude

relatedly, my friend Sergei tells
me how torn up he is about a man
actually named Achilles

whom he met last winter at the sauna after a swim
and how god had blessed this man in all but one part

(brown skin,
soft stomach-hair

ram-eyed, part Indian
part German, square
yet round—)

my friend, surrounded by lasers and mist
in the club—I reach for his hips, the smell
of the club incisive and muscular

and his hips are tied
and at the end of the rope is the door of the sauna
the knob too hot to grasp, like the closet that holds the holy books:

"He flew back to Germany, I miss him so much"

Major Content

the house is cold
because

the door is open
and the windows
are failing

also, now
is a time of changes

I go back to our game

your pawn will take my rook
unless

I threaten
your queen

the question is
do this with the knight
or with the bishop

both of which are safe
so long as your bishop stays
between my queen
and yours

a threat like this
is a threat only
formal

in a world of rules
and devices

unlike the lawn game
from Switzerland

four blocks of wood
on each side
and a kingpin
in the center

the objective being
to be the first
to knock the kingpin down
by tossing a set of sticks

outside, the wind sanctions
the travel of small things

leaves are blown in
shriveled and peculiar
to gather in a terminus
around the toilet

here it is
a portion of the world

not a form
but such a quantity
of pressure as will
compel the leaves

so that the leaves continue
to collect

and the door to the garden
yawns open

in the end I decide on the bishop
but I've ignored something

not in the yard
or on the table

something you said
years ago
while we were driving

though that seems less important now
than what had prompted you to speak

the road lay smooth
curved everywhere

a thousand exits and stations
all of them leading back to the house

a holiday light
filtering to every room

closing the books
quenching the lily
in its pot

putting the pieces back
in their first position

the pawns arranged
below the court

the grid comprising
a difference
of opposing forces
equal in number
equal in power

and the floor between them
on which the pieces fall
one after another

into the truth
the end of the analysis
"check mate"

Contrapposto

the pool locker room
as a kind of museum
a room of nude strangers
tall and muscular
chatting or going quietly
drying their chests
or dressing or undressing
adjusting
their trunks or handling
a blow dryer or frowning
in a mirror

the next day
you bring me a sandwich
from the kitchen
and put on Madonna
we haven't listened
to Madonna
since February
she's so good

all day I read
a book, finish
your Camels
and search
for words
I've made
a start of it
and now

can see
the evening beginning
the starry decoy
cruising
in the blue park
where you go walking
life trailing behind you
like a sad ad
attached
to a small plane

in which
a gorgeous man
promoting underwear
lies sprayed with dew
like a specimen
in a greenhouse

and what
if now I leaned
out our window
to whistle
to the neighbor's son
outside, in long underwear
in autumn, keen
as a knife
climbing through
his window

after a night
of drinking?

would I fall?
would love
set me carefully
down on the street
and let me wander?
how far could I go?
how often leave
the apartment
and still feel
those mellow shoulders
pull me back
with that notorious
unsuspected
strength of theirs?

Circuit Studies

1.
Reflection begins after the party …

when cigarettes are passed around on little trays.
The same person in the casket as before
the same gray court out in front
the wind and fleeing shapes, the shape for instance
of a giant wheel, the wheel of the estate.

It may look like a city,
but it is the desert.

A woman at a cafe
gazes bitterly at her salad.
I know her, I think to myself.

To establish the second life,
we give up the first.
But the first must once have been
just like the second.

For now, I sit and chat with friends: this guy is alright,
that guy is not so good. But I like his poetry. Young men
in charming clothes: a red sweater, corduroy trousers
green suede jacket and jeans
blue turtleneck and a yellow cap,
silk scarf and Reeboks, deferring,
deferring, and going over what

we can remember today, and going back
there and going for more,

in the loop of conversation,
where the forgotten casually
reemerges,

I sit up in the casket with my thought.

2.
A sign on the highway

it's California
the hills succeed
each other.

We arrive at a skyless night
on a porch overlooking the valley
we discuss the present.

Then we hear the voice of the nation
on the television descending
through static:

Oh lovely nation
Oh sunny little nation
Oh nation doing well

We leave the doom of conversation
and go inside,

the cats asleep on the piano
the dog lying in the doorway
blocking the doorway

the rooms the kitchen the furniture
vivid partitions—

in a painting over the sofa
the Maenads tear apart prince Pentheus.

A fly cruises into an outlet.

Is it extinguished, or
does it come out
on the other side
at the banquet of the afterlife?

3.
A car pulls up to a curb
inside it a flock of birds

the sky today rainy and wounded
the poem an intent to stab.

I will spend tomorrow in the city
playing checkers in my father's store.

I call Gianni, he reminds me, years ago on his birthday at the Met
of paintings by George Grosz and Max Beckmann.
How does he remember?

Grosz's pale figures
the bourgeois fat and red
the women stringy
the intellectuals ashen, green

and Beckmann's ruined parlors ...

I meet Gianni at the bar
where the beer is "cold as your ex's heart"

and the Saints lose three players on their offensive line
before halftime.
It is terrible.

The helmeted players move in slow motion on the screen
and gradually the game is made sense of
the pass reviewed—

neither the players, nor the referee, nor the spectators
decide the outcome.

Everyone waits and counts
as if the final score
were something they'd forgotten
and the game, only a means of remembering it.

4.
O show me
the way around it

the back
of the trick card

and the errors
of predecessors ...

I sit in the professor's office,
a fan turns idly by a brass window
and a parrot, also called professor,
stands by in a cage.

On the table
a heavy book is open:
Allegories

In a caved in
huge old armchair
he begins to talk

of tenure
and the function of the scholar.

The perfect scholar, he says,
will know nothing.

With nothing,
he can return to the old knowledge,
which is all but lost to us.

Uri Rosenshine

The Regime

in comes the ghost to complain
of its unhappy union with the communities
of the living

Abraham Teixeira
son of João Pedro Teixeira
leader of the peasant league
is killed by the regime
on the road leading from Sapé

tears filling his beard
and waving a fist he says
let it be recorded—let it be recorded
that we are against all systems
no system helps the poor

his old mother beside him vigorously nodding
why do we no longer hear of the We?
they are all dead like my husband
so we talk of justice
but we no longer say revolution
the word that is like bread

cypress trees emerge
above a stony ridge
a ruined house
where no one sleeps
a broken fridge

I wander down a pathway
like a wheel on a string
to render my report

tall shrubs and old machines
the flesh of trees
the silver air and colorless leaves

the sun is sitting in the sky
like a statement in a rock—a promise
frozen till it is fulfilled

I say, let there be no dogma—
I dogmatize

there's the prison
the razor and the mirror as they were left
the wire chairs in the little plaza

the pit where at gunpoint
musicians deposited their horns
and scholars their glasses
the mantle where the general installed his picture

if we outpace this dream
and wake from the regime

shaking off a beard of tears
what will we see?

a pack of shiny birds
soaring in a V across
a liberal sky
an emblem of the We?

looking down, I find a bullet in my chest
I go around talking with strangers
smoothly, relaxed *I've been shot—I'm dying*
Here, look I say, showing it off

I find my way to the apartment
I shower and apply cologne
I water the plants, feed the parrot
even have a smoke on the balcony
I meet friends at a dinner party

there are drinks and a roast
at dessert I finally expire
in the middle of telling the joke
about an old woman who smokes in the rain
using condoms

my face white and my torso washed in blood

II

Domestic Scene

the roofs are nice
spangled with rain
we watch the episode
on crocodiles again

outside the crocodiles
sleeping in the park
remember the Euphrates
and its eucalyptus

we have vodka with brunch
in front of the tennis match
the crocodiles stir
each time a point is scored

and when the dial swerves
the game is over
we exit to the sandy street
where there are houses

each has its own fruit tree
and a tile hallway
that is daily washed
at the end of which

one can see a courtyard
concealed from the world
that light reaches
but not wind

Uri Rosenshine

within are a broom
a dustpan and a stool
a pile of leaves beneath a ficus
and a bird who recites phrases

the opening to the sky
held up by beams
is like a gate to a wilderness
swinging loose

when we turn back
the evening has arrived
the first stars appear
above the dark roofs

The Chariot

on the drive into the city
you pass me a hash cigarette
put on Selda
the Turkish singer-dissident
and tacitly forbid me to read

I'm sorry I was so late
I was talking with friends
sharing news at the end
of a long week

but you have a way of according
to your own habits a special dignity
they do not themselves merit
you want to be complimented for buying milk
or seeing a new movie

I will not speak with you
if I cannot read

when we get to a garden party
for a lesbian wedding
we're finally allowed to relax

your friends admire me
because I am younger than they
and because somehow this time
I have succeeded in showing them
how harmless I am

one is so shy
he tells me about a fight with his new wife
and about a new house in Astoria
which his parents will renovate for him embarrassingly
while he prolongs a honeymoon in Japan
I love him immediately
but this will be kept a secret

you hold me in my sleep
and if I speak in my sleep
into the damp canal
I hear it speaking back
but with the meaning clear

oh, if I could speak to it again
my sex approaching blindly
from a distant room
you hovering near
resourcefully ...

you are right on time
I kiss your stomach and your chest
it is like walking around in Jerusalem
watching dark Arab boys pass
through the courtyard, sweating
in white linen, moving furniture for Jews

we have figs and yogurt for breakfast
and go down to the market

where they are selling snakes
and replica Tower-of-Davids

an armoire with precious inlays
floats by us, carried from behind
by a pair of young men in sandals
as if transporting itself
it depicts the assumption of Elijah
on a fiery chariot, his servant
clutching his mother-of-pearl mantle as he ascends
unwilling to part from his master

The Seaport Painting

if you go out into the wilderness
and sleep there
striving among the animals
eluding the more dominant
improvising shelter

Pan will not take interest in you
the hermit will not quit his hiding place

but one night drinking with friends
in the city where you grew up
you will notice a strange man
talking and drinking at a prominent table

in all his movements you will recognize
the cunning of the animal

everything will indicate danger
as you hoped when you began
everything will have a purpose

*

in my mother's painting
of winter at the seaport

is an underpass
leading to the docks

in the narrow place
is a dark window

where vendors were
in September

now, a thin light
of great delicacy

hesitantly painted
is reflected on it

so that the pass seems
to turn, unexpectedly

going left
away from the docks

the pathway
to the city of the dead

*

my grandmother is visiting
and we are all fasting

I hope that life is not this
a long delirium

Uri Rosenshine

I pick up a magazine
in an ad for Gucci

a man wearing red lace shorts
and a baby-blue turtleneck sweater

rides a skateboard through an empty mall
past an indoor flower shop in Germany

*

you will watch the famous predator
as he passes through your life, this once

how you have underestimated yourself
he will say

you thought yourself capable of little
and so you made little

and now the wilderness seems to return
the wilderness which, I remember
you promised, would never return
now seems to return

Dichotomy

I spend all day deliberating
to whom these flowers should go
white anemones late-blooming

one friend in the hospital
unable to eat

and one at home
with whom I share a bed

*

I tell jokes on the way to the hospital
eager to see my unhappy friend

high on morphine
taking visitors and dispensing insight
watching the contents of his stomach
as they travel up a tube
to a small receptacle
where they come to rest

he is bright and noble

*

half asleep in the garden
it is unusually warm for September
I get up to look for my boyfriend

here he is sleeping beside the fountain
halfway beneath a rhododendron
breathing peacefully
a breeze in his hair

his black expressive hair
and his amphibian face

both odd and precious
gleaming foreignly in the fountain basin

someone has thrown a jacket
over him, to cover him

thank you for minding him,
whoever you are

my commerce with him is dangerous
and long-term

every day he tries to lead me astray
so I must always keep a step ahead

and the more that I love him
the more I call him enemy and stranger

Native Realm

I spend all week and the weekend
doing things for others

handing my life out to them

they seem to have a claim on it
but the need to honor such claims

is a half-need
promise made in a dream

when I get home
my friends are all asleep
and my sexual partner indefinitely on holiday

what do I do with myself?

the angel of isolation is standing in the kitchen
waiting near the microwave
he has helped himself to a beer

the last time I saw him I was a child
we were smoking together in Moulmein
on the temple balcony overlooking the prison

plaster animals all around us
the monkey and the rhinoceros
dancing on the banister

the prison, tall and crumbling
made of soft pink brick and surrounded
by blossoming frangipani trees

the dusty street where chickens
and little goats wandered

and maidens walked under parasols
and barbers slept in their dark stalls

later I got a haircut
and we walked along the flat hazy river
and watched the thin canoes sliding in the water
shuddering with speed
the pilot sitting low in the vessel, unseen
and the oars rising and dipping against the sun

how did you find me here, I ask him
did I leave some trace of myself
when I fled from you, when I left
in search of peers
and a reputation?

you forgot this, he answers
and produces a piece
of folded paper

among a web of creases
it is simply written:
do not forget

Uri Rosenshine

Der Schein

1.
a day of rain

I, an asthmatic,
stay in the apartment

today is the first day
I'm not behind

I wake up early
and my work is easy

when it ends
I enter into bed
with dirty feet

watch the bad weather play out

in high school
I had my first real feeling
for a friend

it followed, I believe
the discovery

of the effect of words

when he said of the weather
it's wet

it ceased to be wet
birds emerged

and a white fire
around his black hair

2.
working in the philosophical city
with its ruins and its marketplace

the streets of the peasant quarter
curling inward

concealing an artifact they still use, not knowing its name

and past that the marketplace
where they debate to the point of violence

and past that the icy river

I see the white pale bases of pillars
gleaming in the mental night, on the Athenian hill

in the house of Agathon
they're having a party

the most beautiful boy I know of
is lying there on a wooden bench, half clothed

black curls fall round his ears
and a tin crown rests
upon his head

he will never move from there

Athens is gone
suppressed by another Athens

but in a text from Plato
he remains, blushing

calmly ecstatic
as a long night of wine and chatter
reaches an end

3.
I awoke, ready for the century
apple blossoms and columbine at my window

in my books
insight is suffocated by procedure

I prefer music and marijuana
the club and the spa
the views of a familiar city
the opportunity for fame and disgrace

4.
the leaves a banner
"appearances"

shade falling on the bedroom wall

the act of reading
gives life a sense of form

but this sense is our own doing
which experience repeals

eventually, however
experience falls away

and the form stands alone

The Planet

I have seen it all my life
but I have never sat down and watched it
pea-colored and pied

amazing
it moves without my help

rising when the moon is down
evoking another time

I look into the shadow
of an old green wall and find
nasturtiums, pale, revolving

like a painting of Ingres'
of a woman involved in bathing
behind a wall

I search a ditch and glean
from the dry grass
gleaming

how, passing through the zone
one finds what one is lacking

The Rhinoceros

his horn is beautiful
many desire it

but it is protected by law

the public adores him
because he is large
free and alone

but he is dangerous
because he is impulsive

in his happy dance
he plays out in advance
the end of his career

they hardly notice
the large body
covered with dirt
brushed by flies

they see only the horn
moving on its own …

remember the year
he danced in Marrakech
on the wet shore

miming the palms
with his shoulders

and the sea-moon
with his horn?

he seemed so light
and small

mocking the princess of Morocco
in sandals and a veil ...

remember what happened later
at the banquet?

the servants placed him
behind a hanging carpet

so that only the horn
could be seen

Macau

as if at the Macau ferry terminal
watching the light diminish on departing vessels
across from the Sands Casino
with its great sign and wheel-of-fire
dispersing red light on black water

awaiting no one
apart from the cycle of visitors
the hour of tourism falls away
and the world that is devoted to it
can be seen for the first time

I begin walking toward a guesthouse
in the place of paper lanterns

past the emerald parlors
and the gambling halls
where countless chips have blown
down velvet wells
and a million millionaires
have been depleted by the roulettes

the tables sink down in the dark

for a moment
I can understand the Mandarin:

Heaven is fortuitous
Serve heaven with wise conduct

heaven means power
and fortuitous means prosperous

Power is prosperous
Serve power with great gambling

but heaven also means the void
and fortuitous also means random or haphazard

The void is hazardous
Serve the void with discretion

I pass the shipyard and the refineries
where the power tower blinks on and off
to alert the airplanes of its existence

when I come to the place of paper lanterns
the floor is swept, the hammock is free
and the tamarind tree is well-tended

the void is prosperous
there are no signs to give direction
there are no shuttles or ferries
and no guests walking up and down
there is no gong to start the games
no mimic, no speeches

the lanterns are floating high, unwrapping,
the true night of Macau is showing itself at last

it is the high priestess of the first dynasty
putting on her single-threaded gown, she
who scattered stalks of yarrow
to read her heart's changes,
in her nightly preparation for sleep

Vaccine

in childhood you lived in a public park
with a she-wolf pacing heavily there
in a dress of rancid hair, in the high grass,
larger than a man

the fear of her brought you into the world
where every child is alike
where daylight, games and classroom chants
were thought to keep the wolf abroad

the complexity of good behavior
gradually immured you to the fear
but holiday or sickness could
by interrupting the defensive trance
bring back a carnal fragrance,
sweetness, special to her breath

those that did not cross beyond
the boundary of childhood
were not so much spared the trouble of this fear
as taken back, into that dimmest
and most pleasant memory of seclusion

while those that advanced
did so by forgetting the early phase,
both the ungoverned pasture
and its hidden governess

later, when drugs emerge as a form of play,
inflaming the nerves, darkening the vision,
it is as if to keep the she-wolf near

Enthusiasm

six days alone with my dad in the city
I smoke a spliff and go to the Met
where for the first time I love Rembrandt
his self-portrait
the face conveying a world
of vigorous intelligence in action
that dwindles into sanity and manliness
and his *Noble Slav*
and his *Aristotle with the Bust of Homer*

I go home through the park and look at boys
I also pass a butterfly bush, balloon flowers, echinacea
open water poppies in the fountain under a magnolia
a bronze statue of a god with a reed-flute
as at the Met the Bacchus in marble, sitting on a tiger
dangling a pack of marble grapes

at home I listen to Little Richard and watch porn
big catholic cocks, my amateurs—
Life is a bright gate, open to all

my dad comes home with pork ribs and bourbon
his face perversely glowing, as if moonlit

how capable he is now
brooding and being cheerful at the same time

how like one of those Spanish skeletons
arriving in the evening
at the famous town ruined by plague

appreciating the odor of the carcasses
the late sunlight in a desolate place
the sand whirling in the street
the gray dog starving slowly in the purple grass
the houses full of shadow seeming to wilt

and waving his hands expressly (being an actor)
admiring or pretending to admire

giving these things due poignancy,
due glow in the time of their final change

Finding Nemo

most of the year you live peacefully
surrounded by friends
each has a special neurosis and charm
and a job equal to his skill

yellow sand as your floor
small caverns cloaked in pretty barnacles
pathways walled by seagrass
and a view of the window
a view of the ocean
glimmering and flat
entering Sydney Harbor

no one minds that this world is bound
by glass, and maintained
by gloved hands from above

except when you are harassed
by a giant redheaded girl
who chooses one of you
to amuse herself with
until he tires out
and is discarded

so that no bond can develop among you
no project that is not overshadowed
by absurd danger

a net descends
pursues the chosen one
brings him up through the surface

then you lament your bound village
and wish for transport somehow
to the waters of the harbor
where though the danger is constant
it isn't certain, there being always
more ocean, the chance of escape

but it is impossible
between this place and the harbor
there are no channels

so you devise something higher
a piece of intellect to leverage your predicament

all this, you say, *the rocking grass*
the sandy paths, is an illusion
contrived by the redheaded girl's uncle
to detain me here, a sacrifice to her

my true self is in the harbor
nothing frightens him
he comes and goes as he likes

a great accident tore us apart
swimming outside the reef
I saw a giant diver
and was taken away

perhaps the diver loved my colors
my orange head
and my black and white sides
perhaps he thought
that I was something else
no matter

I see the bubbles going to escape
trapped spheres of air
I know it is all held together by a little machine:
a tube with a filter and a spinning blade

Minutiae

To the high place, upon ice,
in which my man lives
daintily.

A heated room.
Plants, cushions.
Glass containers.
Minutiae.

Pebbles, bits of textile.
Pictures cut
from fashion magazines.

Marbles, representing planets,
suspended in translucent glycerine.

I cross the snow,
the sky a cabinet
of silver pieces,
that move,
with hooks, handles
and grooves,
in ways determined
by their shapes.

All is provisional with me.
Suppose I'm late to the loft.
Suppose I send the friends

away. In the time when all is silent
and a cloud covers Arcturus.

All is only scenery,
a handy condition
that nature provides
that something large
and broadly useful, something energetic
may be built,

provided it be something also rugged
and attractive.

Something like a bell
with some magnanimous saint
graven on it—St. George

who plays sports
and does not hesitate
to thrust his pike
at pretty crocodiles.

Hey! Someone calls me.
I look up to see a head in a window
that seems to have opened in the sky.

Here I am, I say.
I can't see you, he replies.

It is after midnight. It is cold.
How long will it take you to get up here?

It is not so cold, I say.
But I am coming. I will be there soon.

I'm going to bed, he says.
I have to work in the morning.

And draws his head inside.

Acknowledgements

I am indebted to the editors of the following publications, where poems were originally published:

The Missouri Review: "The Regime"

Right Hand Pointing: "Monadology" (formerly titled "Reader")

Tofu Ink Arts Press: "The Tea Stall"

Sortes Magazine: "Lotus," "The Parrot," "Invitation to Vermont," "Monadology," and "Modest Forecast" (formerly titled "Presentiment of Disappointment")

The Journal of Undiscovered Poets: "Dichotomy"

Emory Lullwater Review: "Contrapposto"

Poetica Magazine: "Chagallig"

Tikkun Magazine: "The Surface Circus"

Writers in the Know: "Minutiae"

The New Note Poetry Magazine: "The Seaport Painting"

I also wish to thank Louise Glück for her guidance and encouragement, and Kenny and my family for their constant support.

About the Author

URI ROSENSHINE was born in Jerusalem and raised in New York City. He studied mixed media sculpture at The Art Students League of New York before going on to pursue an bachelor's degree at Yale. There he completed a thesis in verse writing under Louise Glück and a thesis in philosophy with a focus on German Idealism and aesthetics under Martin Hägglund. He continues to reside in New Haven, Connecticut, where he works at a wine store and indulges in miscellaneous pursuits such as bookbinding and gardening. He draws inspiration for writing from the visual arts and philosophy, from his day job and the weather, and from his friends and family. He is passionate about the processes of composition and revision, and has hopes of becoming a full time writer. His first chapbook, *Minutiae*, was self-published in collaboration with Directangle Press and hand-bound by the author.

www.ingramcontent.com/pod-product-compliance
Lightning Source LLC
Chambersburg PA
CBHW021425090426
42742CB00009B/1266